A Note to Parents

Dorling Kindersley *Readers* is a compelling new program for beginning readers, designed in conjunction with leading literacy experts, including Dr. Linda Gambrell, President of the National Reading Conference and past board member of the International Reading Association.

Beautiful illustrations and superb full-color photographs combine with engaging, easy-to-read stories to offer a fresh approach to each subject in the series. Each Dorling Kindersley *Reader* is guaranteed to capture a child's interest while developing his or her reading skills, general knowledge, and love of reading.

The four levels of Dorling Kindersley *Readers* are aimed at different reading abilities, enabling you to choose the books that are exactly right for your child:

Level 1 for **Preschool to Grade 1**
Level 2 for **Grades 1 to 3**
Level 3 for **Grades 2 and 3**
Level 4 for **Grades 2 to 4**

The "normal" age at which a child begins to read can be anywhere from three to eight years old, so these levels are intended only as a general guideline.

No matter which level you select, you can be sure that you are helping your child learn to read, then read to learn!

D1018618

Dorling  Kindersley

LONDON, NEW YORK, SYDNEY, DELHI, PARIS,
MUNICH and JOHANNESBURG

Produced by NFL Publishing Group
Vice President/Editor in Chief
John Wiebusch
Managing Editor Chuck Garrity, Sr.
Project Editor James Buckley, Jr.
Art Director Bill Madrid
Designer Helen Choy Whang

For DK Publishing
Editor Regina Kahney
Reading Consultant
Linda Gambrell, Ph.D.

First American Edition, 2000
Published in the United States by
Dorling Kindersley, Inc.
95 Madison Ave., New York, NY 10016

2 4 6 8 10 9 7 5 3 1

Library of Congress Catalog #00-024793

ISBN 0-7894-6378-4 (hc)
ISBN 0-7894-6757-7 (pb)

Printed in China

All Photographs are Copyright © NFL Photos.
l=left, r=right, FC=front cover
The Allens: 16, 21, 28; **Rob Brown:** 18;
Michael Burr: 15, 29, 39, 44, 47; **Jimmy Cribb:** FC, 37;
Dave Cross: 35; **Bill Cummings:** 7; **Malcolm Emmons:**
FC; **Andy Hayt:** 12; **Paul Jasienski:** 27; **Allen Kee:** 46;
John McDonough: 10; **Al Messerschmidt:** 22, 27r, 40;
Roger Motzkus (illus.): 11; **NFL Photos/Paul Spinelli:**
30, 34, 36, 38; **Rich Pilling:** 17, 26l;
Pro Football Hall of Fame: 19; **Bob Rosato:** 8, 14, 32;
Tony Tomsic: 31; **Corky Trewin:** 4;
Michael Zagaris: FC, 24, 25, 33, 45; **Joel Zwink:** 42.

see our complete
catalog at
www.dk.com

Contents

DORLING KINDERSLEY *READERS*

READING **3** ALONE

SUPER BOWL
HEROES

Written by James Buckley, Jr.

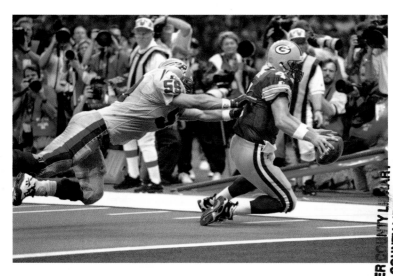

A Dorling Kindersley Book

Joe Montana led the 49ers to four Super Bowl titles.

Hero time

As the end of the Super Bowl game nears, thousands of fans in the stadium scream and shout. Millions more people watching the game on TV are on the edge of their seats.

The Super Bowl is the championship of the National Football League (NFL). It is played every year in late January between the two best NFL teams.

Often, the winner of the Super Bowl is led by a great quarterback.

Quarterbacks use great football skills to lead their team to victory. But many players have great football skills. So what makes a hero?

A Super Bowl hero is different because he comes through when his team—and their fans—need him most.

Super Joe

San Francisco 49ers quarterback Joe Montana looked up at the scoreboard. It read: Cincinnati 16, San Francisco 13. The scoreboard also showed that three and a half minutes remained in Super Bowl XXIII in 1989. Joe's team was behind by three points, and the game was on the line.

It was up to him to lead the 49ers to victory.

"Okay, guys," he said, clapping his hands as they gathered together in the huddle. "Here we go."

Counting Super Bowls
Super Bowls are counted using Roman numerals.
I = 1; V = 5; X = 10.

In the next three and a half minutes,
Montana became a Super Bowl hero.
Starting from the 49ers' 8-yard line,
Montana and his teammates began a
drive into Super Bowl history.

Montana was the center of attention at Super Bowl XXIII.

Montana led the team down the field. He attempted 9 passes and completed 8 of them.

During the team's thrilling drive, Montana impressed his teammates with his cool leadership under fire.

At one point, he looked up from the huddle. "Hey, guys, look at that," he said. He pointed out John Candy, an actor and comedian, sitting in the stands. Then he went back to work.

Finally, the 49ers reached the Cincinnati 10-yard line. Montana called a play intended for running back Roger Craig. Or Montana could go to John Taylor across the middle.

The two teams faced each other across the line of scrimmage with the Super Bowl at stake.

The noise was incredible as the fans roared. All eyes were on Joe.

Montana took the snap and dropped back to pass. His blockers stopped the Bengals, giving him time to throw.

He saw that Craig was covered. So he went to his second option. Montana waited until Taylor broke free, then rifled a pass toward the end zone!

Taylor caught it with only 34 seconds left in the game. Touchdown, 49ers! San Francisco was the NFL champion.

Snap
To start every play, the center (right) hands the ball through his legs to the quarterback (16). This is called the "snap."

"When you're a kid playing in your backyard, you always win the Super Bowl on the last play," Montana said. "To have that come true...that was fun."

But Montana was used to being a Super Bowl hero. He was named the game's most valuable player (MVP) three times. He helped the 49ers win four Super Bowls.

Montana wasn't the best passer or the fastest runner. What made Montana a hero was the confidence he had in himself to win no matter what.

In January 1982, seven years before his winning pass to Taylor, Montana had his first chance to be a Super Bowl hero. The 49ers also faced the Cincinnati Bengals in Super Bowl XVI.

Montana and teammate Randy Cross celebrate another victory.

Montana was in control of the game
from the opening kickoff. Under his
leadership, the 49ers jumped out to a
20-0 lead. He scored on a 1-yard run.

He passed to running back Earl Cooper for another touchdown.

The Bengals had a strong defense, but Montana had no trouble finding his receivers. San Francisco carefully mixed running and passing plays and controlled the ball.

In the second half, the Bengals bounced back, coming as close as 20-14. But Montana led two more drives that ended in field goals for the 49ers. The final score was San Francisco 26, Cincinnati 21. Montana was named the MVP of the game.

Rozelle Trophy
Super Bowl MVPs get this trophy, named for Pete Rozelle, who was Commissioner of the NFL from 1960 to 1989.

Three years later, in 1985, the 49ers were in the Super Bowl again, this time against the Miami Dolphins. Miami had

a passing star of its own in Dan Marino. In only his second NFL season, Marino had thrown an NFL-record 48 touchdown passes. Could Montana and the 49ers outscore the record-breaking Dolphins?

Montana quickly proved that the 49ers could. He passed for three touchdowns in the game, and scored on a 6-yard touchdown run. The 49ers' defense shut down the Dolphins' powerful attack, and San Francisco cruised to a 38-16 victory.

Montana earned his second Super Bowl MVP award. The 49ers set a record with 537 total yards. The old pro had outplayed the hot young passer.

Montana's final Super Bowl success came in January 1990, in Super Bowl XXIV. With three titles under his belt, Montana made this fourth one look easy. He passed for a Super Bowl-record five touchdowns, and helped the 49ers set a record for points scored. The final score was San Francisco 55, Denver 10.

In nine years, Joe Montana led his team to four Super Bowls, and he helped the 49ers win all four. He won three MVP trophies, more than any other player.

Montana strikes a familiar pose—signaling another 49ers touchdown.

He holds all-time Super Bowl records for passer rating, passing yards, completions, and touchdown passes.

"It's different going out on the field for the Super Bowl," Montana says today. "It's the way your hair stands up on the back of your neck and your arms. It was almost like you weren't even walking, you were floating."

For these and many other successes, Montana was voted into the Pro Football Hall of Fame in January 2000.

Pro Football Hall of Fame
This building in Canton, Ohio, houses football memorabilia and honors the game's greatest players.

On his shoulders

What was the big story heading into Super Bowl XXII in January 1988? Was it the Redskins making their third Super Bowl appearance of the 1980s? Was it the Denver Broncos playing in their second consecutive Super Bowl?

No. Before the game, everyone was talking about Doug Williams, the Redskins' quarterback.

Williams certainly was a great passer and a top-notch leader. But the reason everyone was talking about Williams was that he was an African-American. No black quarterback had ever led his team to a Super Bowl.

Doug was aware of all the talk, but he knew that it wouldn't matter once the game began.

Williams was the center of attention for reporters at Super Bowl XXII.

Fritz Pollard

Several African-American players were part of the NFL in its early days. Fritz Pollard was a player and coach for several teams.

Williams calmly answered all the questions from reporters during the week before the game.

"The Redskins didn't hire me to be the first black quarterback in the Super Bowl," he said. "They hired me to help them win it."

Although Williams seemed calm outside, he knew that he would be a model for future black quarterbacks if he succeeded. He also would be an excuse for teams *not* to hire black quarterbacks in the future if he failed.

Something happened early in the game that almost meant failure for the Redskins. In the first quarter, Williams slipped and hurt his left knee.

Was the game over for Williams? Would his injury shatter his dream?

As Williams watched teammate Jay Schroeder take his place, he knew that he had to get back into the game.

Coach Joe Gibbs came over and asked Doug how he felt.

"I'm okay, coach," Williams said. "It's nothing."

"Okay, then, Douglas," Gibbs said. "Let's get rolling."

The crowd roared when Williams limped back onto the field a few moments later. On his first play, early in the second quarter, Williams launched a bomb to Ricky Sanders. The play covered 80 yards. Touchdown, Washington!

The fun was just starting for the Redskins and their fans.

Four minutes later, Williams tossed a 27-yard touchdown pass to Gary Clark.

Gary Clark

Soon after, running back Timmy Smith ran 58 yards for another Redskins' touchdown. In the game, Smith ran for a Super Bowl-record 204 yards.

Timmy Smith

Williams was not done, however. With less than four minutes remaining in the first half, he hooked up with

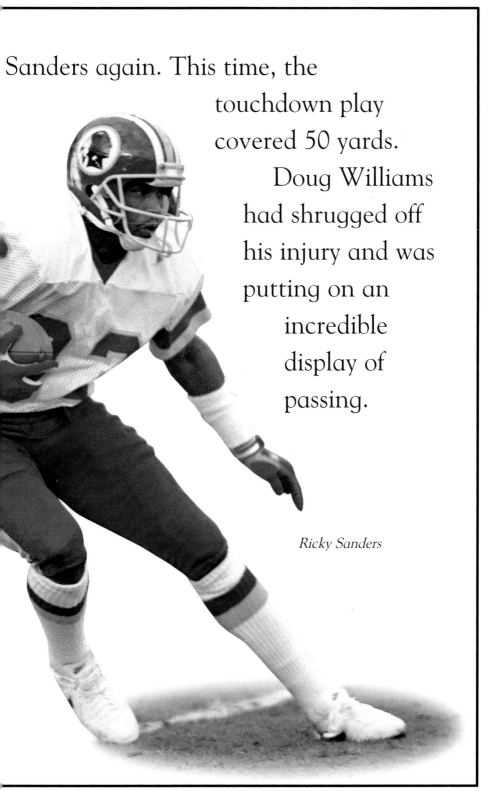

Sanders again. This time, the touchdown play covered 50 yards.

Doug Williams had shrugged off his injury and was putting on an incredible display of passing.

Ricky Sanders

Williams raised his hands in victory after the Redskins' triumph.

Finally, Williams threw an 8-yard touchdown pass to tight end Clint Didier. It was his fourth touchdown pass of the quarter. Washington scored 35 points in 15 minutes. Williams had ignored the pressure and succeeded.

With a halftime score of 35-10, the Redskins cruised to a 42-10 victory over the Denver Broncos.

After the game, Williams was named the most valuable player. Later, he was featured on boxes of cereal.

"It was like, for one day, everything I worked for in my life came together," Williams says. "I'm proud of that, proud of what it meant. I felt like it was my job to hold up my end of the deal. I did the job."

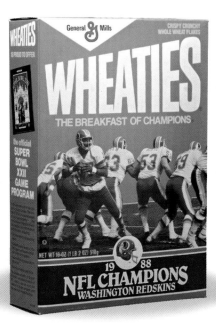

A valuable Super Bowl XXII collectible.

The Pack is back

The Green Bay Packers playing in the Super Bowl was not that surprising...if the year was 1967. But this was 1997 and the Packers had not been to the big game in 29 years.

The man who led Green Bay back to the Super Bowl was a young quarterback nicknamed "Country," who had grown up in a small town called Kiln, Mississippi.

Brett Favre [FARV] had a rifle arm and an ability to make something out of nothing.

Vince Lombardi

Lombardi coached the Packers to five NFL titles in the 1960s. He also led them to victory in Super Bowls I and II.

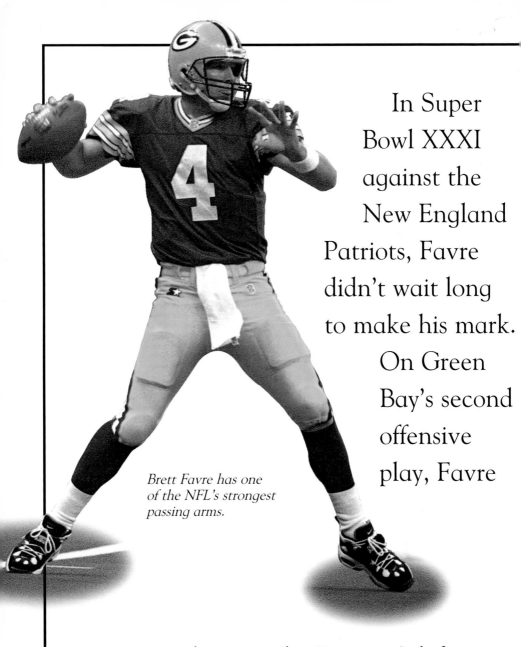

Brett Favre has one
of the NFL's strongest
passing arms.

In Super Bowl XXXI against the New England Patriots, Favre didn't wait long to make his mark. On Green Bay's second offensive play, Favre saw something in the Patriots' defense that made him smile. He called an audible, which means that he changed the play at the last second.

He took the snap, dropped back, and lofted a perfect pass to Andre Rison, who streaked under the ball and caught it for a 54-yard touchdown!

The Pack was back!

But New England had a good young quarterback of its own in Drew Bledsoe. He led his team to two quick scores. Suddenly, Favre and Green Bay trailed 14-10.

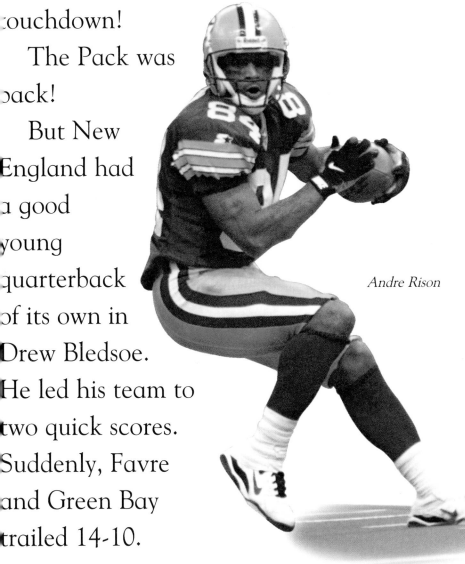

Andre Rison

Early in the second quarter, Favre again made something out of nothing. He spotted a Patriots' defender out of position and waited for receiver Antonio Freeman to take advantage.

Freeman and Favre were on the same page mentally. Freeman caught Favre's pass along the right sideline. Freeman scored on a Super Bowl-record 81-yard touchdown play.

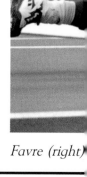

Favre (right)

After a field goal by Green Bay's Chris Jacke, Favre again came through. With less than two minutes left in the half, he ended a long drive by diving in from the 2-yard line for the score.

The Packers had turned the Patriots' 14-10 lead into a 27-14 lead of their own.

get the ball over the goal line for a score in the second quarter.

Green Bay's Desmond Howard electrified the crowd at the Louisiana Superdome with a 99-yard kickoff return for a touchdown. Favre capped off the scoring by completing a pass to Mark Chmura for a 2-point conversion.

Led by the kid from Mississippi, the Packers cruised to a 35-21 victory.

Favre became a genuine Super Bowl hero by leading his fabled team back to the top of the NFL. One of the most memorable sights from the game was seeing the big, tough quarterback run off the field after a big play.

He was holding his helmet over his head and screaming with joy—just like a kid from the country.

Finally, a winner

If John Elway had retired after the 1996 season, he would have been remembered for a great NFL career. He had passed for 300 touchdowns and for thousands of yards. He had earned a reputation for his amazing ability to snatch victory from defeat.

But he had never won a Super Bowl championship. Elway and the Broncos had lost three Super Bowls. But Elway still wanted to try. So he laced up his cleats again for the 1997 season and gave it another shot.

Football cleats
Football players wear leather shoes with hard plastic "cleats" or studs on the bottom for better traction.

In 1997, his fifteenth NFL season, Elway once again led the Broncos to the Super Bowl. They were up against the defending champion Green Bay Packers, led by quarterback Brett Favre.

Before the game, Elway was asked if he would trade all his personal records for a Super Bowl title.

"In a heartbeat," he answered.

The two teams were well matched in the first half. Favre connected with Antonio Freeman on a 22-yard touchdown pass. Then Denver's

great running back Terrell Davis scored on a short run.

Along with having a great passing arm, Elway had always been a good runner throughout his career. He proved it in the Super Bowl when he scored on a 1-yard run.

A great Super Bowl battle was shaping up. At halftime, the score was Denver 17, Green Bay 14.

A Packers' field goal tied the score early in the third quarter. That set the stage for the biggest play of the game, and one of the biggest plays of Elway's long and glorious career.

From the Packers' 12-yard line, Elway dropped back to pass. All his receivers were covered. So he began to run. He needed 6 yards for a key first down, so when he got close, he dived. Three Packers hit him at the same time. Elway, in midair, spun completely around, parallel to the ground.

He landed hard, but he had the first
down. Elway got up and spiked the ball!
    Energized by their leader's grit and
determination, the Broncos scored
moments later to take the lead.

Although the Packers tied it again 24-24, the fired-up Broncos drove right back down the field. With less than two minutes left in the game, Terrell Davis scored on a 1-yard run to make the final score Denver 31, Green Bay 24.

John Elway was finally a champion.

The field filled with celebrating players. A small stage was set up for postgame ceremonies. After Broncos team owner Pat Bowlen accepted the Lombardi Trophy, he held it up to the crowd and pointed to his quarterback.

"This one's for John!"

Lombardi Trophy

The winning team in the Super Bowl receives this silver trophy. It is named for legendary Packers coach Vince Lombardi.

Elway did not stop there, however. He returned for another season in 1998. This time, he and Davis led the Broncos to Super Bowl XXXIII.

The opponent was the Atlanta Falcons. A young Atlanta team was no match for the veteran Broncos. Elway was a master. He passed for 336 yards, including an 80-yard touchdown pass to Rod Smith. Elway also scored on a 3-yard run.

After 16 outstanding seasons, John Elway capped off his career with not one, but two Super Bowl rings and the most-valuable-player trophy.

Then he retired from the NFL—a winner forever.

Glossary

Audible
Occurs when the quarterback calls out or signals to his team to change the play called in the huddle.

First down
The beginning of every offensive series of plays. When the offensive team gains 10 yards in four plays or fewer, it gets a new first down.

Interception
Occurs when a defensive player catches a pass thrown by the offense.

Line of scrimmage
The imaginary line on the field where each play begins. The line moves when a team gains or loses yardage.

National Football League
The 31 professional football teams are divided into the American and National Football Conferences.

Passer rating
Mathematical formula used to compare quarterbacks' statistics.

Playoffs
After the NFL season, the top 12 teams meet in a series of games to determine the league champion.

Quarterback
The most important position on a football team's offense; often calls plays, makes passes.

Snap
When the center hands or tosses the ball backward through his legs to the quarterback.

Spike
Throwing the ball to the ground in celebration of a score or big play.

Super Bowl
The NFL's annual championship game, played each January at a neutral site between the champions of the AFC and the NFC.

Touchdown
Six-point scoring play made by catching the ball in the end zone or running the ball into the end zone.

Touchdown pass
When a quarterback throws the ball to a receiver in the end zone, or when a player catches a pass and then runs into the end zone.